Opening Prayers

Opening Prayers:

Collects in Contemporary Language

*Scripture-related prayers for Sundays and
Holy Days, Years A, B & C*

International Commission
on English in the Liturgy

CANTERBURY
PRESS
Norwich

Liturgical texts from *The Sacramentary,*
Volume One:
Sundays and Feasts
© 1997, International Commission on English in the Liturgy, Inc.
All rights reserved.

First published in hardback in 1999 by
The Canterbury Press Norwich
(a publishing imprint of Hymns Ancient & Modern Limited)
St. Mary's Works, St. Mary's Plain
Norwich, Norfolk, NR3 3BH
This paperback edition issued in 2001

A catalogue record for this book is available
from the British Library

ISBN 1-85311-428-6

Typeset by Regent Typesetting, London
and printed in Great Britain by Biddles Ltd
www.biddles.co.uk

CONTENTS

Holy Week

Season of Easter

Ordinary Time*

Opening Prayers

*NOTE: The Roman Church begins its Ordinary Time from Monday after the First Sunday of Epiphany (the Baptism of the Lord). The Church of England, and other Anglican Churches in the British Isles take Epiphany (tide) through to the Presentation of the Lord (Candlemas) on 2 February and Ordinary Time then runs from 3 February through to Shrove Tuesday inclusive, linking up with the Roman practice again at that point.

PREFACE

As more and more churches have begun to use the Revised Common Lectionary for their Sunday celebrations, there has been an increasing call for worship texts which draw upon and support this lectionary.

The prayers found in this collection were originally prepared by the International Commission on English in the Liturgy for use with the Roman Lectionary (*Ordo Lectionum Missae*), upon which the Revised Common Lectionary is based. The Joint Liturgical Group of Great Britain now commends these prayers so that, alongside the Revised Common Lectionary, they may be readily available to all church users in these islands.

For each Sunday of the year three opening prayer texts are provided. Each is expressly drafted to introduce the set readings of the particular year (A, B or C). In this way the leader of worship is able to provide an orientation for worship based on the scriptures of the day.

Not the least of the benefits of the widespread acceptance of the Revised Common Lectionary has been the realisation that in any village, town or city, more and more Christians are reading the same scriptures at their principal Sunday services. This has strengthened among us the realisation that the scriptures are a major part of our common heritage. In turn it has led many of those responsible for the Sunday proclamation to share in joint Bible study, as the common texts draw them together to a richer and greater understanding of the lively oracles of God.

We now commend these prayers alongside the Revised Common Lectionary as texts which we may use in common. It is our hope that they will give added expression to the growing experience of worship as the activity not simply of the neighbourhood congregation but of the Church universal.

Charles Robertson *Chairman*
Paul Sheppy *Secretary*
Joint Liturgical Group of Great Britain
September, 1998

This first UK edition of Opening Prayers *is dedicated to the memory of the Revd Michael Vasey. He was a member of the Joint Liturgical Group from 1986 to 1998, and longed to see these prayers made available to the churches. He died suddenly, and before the work to bring this about was completed. We are glad now to honour him in this way.*

Collects for Sundays and Holy Days

Years A, B & C

SEASON OF ADVENT

FIRST SUNDAY OF ADVENT

YEAR A

GOD of majesty and power,
    amid the clamour of our violence
your Word of truth resounds;
upon a world made dark by sin
the Sun of Justice casts his dawning rays.

Keep your household watchful
and aware of the hour in which we live.
Hasten the advent of that day
when the sounds of war will be for ever stilled,
the darkness of evil scattered,
and all your children gathered into one.

We ask this through him whose coming is
    certain,
whose day draws near:
your Son, our Lord Jesus Christ,
who lives and reigns with you in the unity of
    the Holy Spirit,
God for ever and ever.

YEAR B

REND the heavens and come down,
    O God of all the ages!
Rouse us from sleep,
deliver us from our heedless ways,
and form us into a watchful people,
that, at the advent of your Son,

he may find us doing what is right,
mindful of all you command.

Grant this through him whose coming is
    certain,
whose day draws near:
your Son, our Lord Jesus Christ,
who lives and reigns with you in the unity of
    the Holy Spirit,
God for ever and ever.

YEAR C GOD our Saviour,
        you utter a word of promise and hope
and hasten the day of justice and freedom,
yet we live in a world forgetful of your word,
our watchfulness dulled by the cares of life.

Keep us alert.
Make us attentive to your word,
ready to look on your Son
when he comes with power and great glory.
Make us holy and blameless,
ready to stand secure
when the day of his coming shakes the world
    with terror.

We ask this through him whose coming is
    certain,
whose day draws near:
your Son, our Lord Jesus Christ,
who lives and reigns with you in the unity of
    the Holy Spirit,
God for ever and ever.

3

SECOND SUNDAY OF ADVENT

YEAR A

YOUR kingdom is at hand,
O God of justice and peace;
you made John the Baptist its herald
to announce the coming of your Christ,
who baptizes with the Holy Spirit and with
fire.

Give us a spirit of repentance
to make us worthy of the kingdom.
Let complacency yield to conviction,
that in our day justice will flourish
and conflict give way
to the peace you bestow in Christ.

Grant this through him whose coming is
certain,
whose day draws near:
your Son, our Lord Jesus Christ,
who lives and reigns with you in the unity of
the Holy Spirit,
God for ever and ever.

YEAR B

WITH tender comfort and transforming
power
you come into our midst,
O God of mercy and might.

Make ready a way in the wilderness,
clear a straight path in our hearts,
and form us into a repentant people,
that the advent of your Son
may find us watchful and eager for the glory
 he reveals.

We ask this through him whose coming is
 certain,
whose day draws near:
your Son, our Lord Jesus Christ,
who lives and reigns with you in the unity of
 the Holy Spirit,
God for ever and ever.

YEAR C GOD of our salvation,
 you straighten the winding ways of our
 hearts
and smooth the paths made rough by sin.

Make our conduct blameless,
keep our hearts watchful in holiness,
and bring to perfection the good you have
 begun in us.

We ask this through him whose coming is
 certain,
whose day draws near:
your Son, our Lord Jesus Christ,
who lives and reigns with you in the unity of
 the Holy Spirit,
God for ever and ever.

THIRD SUNDAY OF ADVENT

YEAR A

GOD of glory and compassion,
at your touch the wilderness blossoms,
broken lives are made whole,
and fearful hearts grow strong in faith.

Open our eyes to your presence
and awaken our hearts to sing your praise.
To all who long for your Son's return
grant perseverance and patience,
that we may announce in word and deed
the good news of the kingdom.

We ask this through him whose coming is
certain,
whose day draws near:
your Son, our Lord Jesus Christ,
who lives and reigns with you in the unity of
the Holy Spirit,
God for ever and ever.

YEAR B

O God, most high and most near,
you send glad tidings to the lowly,
you hide not your face from the poor;
those who dwell in darkness you call into the
light.

Take away our blindness,
remove the hardness of our hearts,
and form us into a humble people,
that, at the advent of your Son,
we may recognize him in our midst
and find joy in his saving presence.

We ask this through him whose coming is
    certain,
whose day draws near:
your Son, our Lord Jesus Christ,
who lives and reigns with you in the unity of
    the Holy Spirit,
God for ever and ever.

YEAR C   ALMIGHTY God,
        you sent your Son into a world
where the wheat must be winnowed from the
    chaff
and evil clings even to what is good.

Let the fire of your Spirit
purge us of greed and deceit,
so that, purified, we may find our peace in you
and you may delight in us.

Grant this through him whose coming is
    certain,
whose day draws near:
your Son, our Lord Jesus Christ,
who lives and reigns with you in the unity of
    the Holy Spirit,
God for ever and ever.

FOURTH SUNDAY OF ADVENT

YEAR A

ETERNAL God,
in the psalms of David,
in the words of the prophets,
in the dream of Joseph
your promise is spoken.
At last, in the womb of the Virgin Mary,
your Word takes flesh.

Teach us to welcome Jesus, the promised
Emmanuel,
and to preach the good news of his coming,
that every age may know him
as the source of redemption and grace.

Grant this through him whose coming is
certain,
whose day draws near:
your Son, our Lord Jesus Christ,
who lives and reigns with you in the unity of
the Holy Spirit,
God for ever and ever.

YEAR B

HERE in our midst, O God of mystery,
you disclose the secret hidden for
countless ages.
For you we wait; for you we listen.

Upon hearing your voice
may we, like Mary, embrace your will
and become a dwelling fit for your Word.

8

Grant this through him whose coming is
    certain,
whose day draws near:
your Son, our Lord Jesus Christ,
who lives and reigns with you in the unity of
    the Holy Spirit,
God for ever and ever.

YEAR C WHO are we, Lord God,
    that you should come to us?
Yet you have visited your people
and redeemed us in your Son.

As we prepare to celebrate his birth,
make our hearts leap for joy at the sound of
    your Word,
and move us by your Spirit to bless your
    wonderful works.

We ask this through him whose coming is
    certain,
whose day draws near:
your Son, our Lord Jesus Christ,
who lives and reigns with you in the unity of
    the Holy Spirit,
God for ever and ever.

SEASON OF CHRISTMAS

25 December

THE BIRTH OF THE LORD

VIGIL MASS

GOD of Abraham and Sarah,
of David and his descendants,
unwearied is your love for us
and steadfast your covenant;
wonderful beyond words
is your gift of the Saviour,
born of the Virgin Mary.

Count us among the people in whom you
delight,
and by this night's marriage of earth and
heaven
draw all generations into the embrace of your
love.

We ask this through Jesus Christ, your Word
made flesh,
who lives and reigns with you in the unity of
the Holy Spirit,
in the splendour of eternal light,
God for ever and ever.

Christmas Day

GOOD and gracious God,
on this holy night you gave us your Son,
the Lord of the universe, wrapped in
   swaddling clothes,
the Saviour of all, lying in a manger.

On this holy night
draw us into the mystery of your love.
Join our voices with the heavenly host,
that we may sing your glory on high.
Give us a place among the shepherds,
that we may find the one for whom we have
   waited,
Jesus Christ, your Word made flesh,
who lives and reigns with you in the unity of
   the Holy Spirit,
in the splendour of eternal light,
God for ever and ever.

MASS AT DAWN

TODAY, O God of light,
your loving kindness dawns,
your tender compassion shines upon us,
for in our Saviour, born of human flesh,
you reveal your gracious gift
of our birth to life eternal.

Fill us with wonder on this holy day:
let us treasure in our hearts
what we have been told,
that our lives may proclaim
your great and gentle mercy.

We ask this through Jesus Christ, your Word
made flesh,
who lives and reigns with you in the unity of
the Holy Spirit,
in the splendour of eternal light,
God for ever and ever.

MASS DURING THE DAY

WE praise you, gracious God,
for the glad tidings of peace,
the good news of salvation:
your Word became flesh,
and we have seen his glory.

Let the radiance of that glory
enlighten the lives
of those who celebrate his birth.

Reveal to all the world
the light no darkness can extinguish,
our Lord Jesus Christ,
who lives and reigns with you in the unity of
the Holy Spirit,
in the splendour of eternal light,
God for ever and ever.

THE HOLY FAMILY

Sunday within the Octave of Christmas

YEAR A

L OVING God,
guardian of our homes,
when you entrusted your Son
to the care of Mary and Joseph,
you did not spare them the pains
that touch the life of every family.

Teach us to rely on your word,
that in our trials as in our joys
we may be clothed in gentleness and patience
and united in love.

Make us ever thankful
for the blessings you give us
through Jesus Christ, your Word made flesh,
who lives and reigns with you in the unity of
the Holy Spirit,
in the splendour of eternal light,
God for ever and ever.

YEAR B

O God,
you cradle us at the beginning of life
and embrace us at our journey's end,
for you love us as your own.

Bind our families together
and deepen our faith,
that, like the Holy Family of Nazareth,
we may grow in wisdom,
obedient to your word.

We ask this through Jesus Christ, your Word
    made flesh,
who lives and reigns with you in the unity of
    the Holy Spirit,
in the splendour of eternal light,
God for ever and ever.

YEAR C

A S your sons and daughters, O loving God,
we come before you in thanksgiving,
called and united by your eternal Word.

Teach us to ponder the mystery of Nazareth,
that we may always find in you
the source of our strength
and the unity of our families.

We ask this through Jesus Christ, your Word
    made flesh,
who lives and reigns with you in the unity of
    the Holy Spirit,
in the splendour of eternal light,
God for ever and ever.

1 JANUARY

MARY, MOTHER OF GOD

MOST high God,
you come near to us this Christmas season
in the child born of the Virgin Mary.
In the depths of darkness, she gave birth to light;
in the depths of silence, she brought forth the Word.

Grant that we who ponder these things in our hearts
may recognize in her child
our Lord and Saviour, Jesus Christ,
who lives and reigns with you in the unity of the Holy Spirit,
in the splendour of eternal light,
God for ever and ever.

SECOND SUNDAY OF CHRISTMAS

G OD most high,
your only Son embraced the weakness of
our flesh
to give us the power to become your children;
your eternal Word chose to dwell among us,
that we might live in your presence.

Grant us a spirit of wisdom
to know how rich is the glory you have made
our own,
and how great the hope to which we are called
in Jesus Christ, your Word made flesh,
who lives and reigns with you in the unity of
the Holy Spirit,
in the splendour of eternal light,
God for ever and ever.

6 JANUARY

THE EPIPHANY OF THE LORD

L ORD God of the nations,
  we have seen the star of your glory
rising in splendour.
The radiance of your incarnate Word
pierces the darkness that covers the earth
and signals the dawn of peace and justice.

Make radiant the lives of your people
with that same brightness,
and beckon all the nations
to walk as one in your light.

We ask this through Jesus Christ, your Word
    made flesh,
who lives and reigns with you in the unity of
    the Holy Spirit,
in the splendour of eternal light,
God for ever and ever.

THE BAPTISM OF THE LORD

(The Sunday between 7 & 13 January inclusive)

YEAR A

GOD of the covenant,
you anointed your beloved Son
with the power of the Holy Spirit,
to be light for the nations
and release for captives.

Grant that we who are born again
of water and the Spirit
may proclaim with our lips the good news of
his peace
and show forth in our lives the victory of his
justice.

We make our prayer through Jesus Christ,
your Word made flesh,
who lives and reigns with you in the unity of
the Holy Spirit,
in the splendour of eternal light,
God for ever and ever.

YEAR B

GOD of salvation,
in the river Jordan you bathed your Son
Jesus in glory
and revealed him as your obedient servant.

In spirit and in power
rend the heavens and come down to us.
Strengthen us to acknowledge your Christ,

that we who are reborn in his likeness
may walk with him the path of obedience.

Grant this through Jesus Christ, your Word
    made flesh,
who lives and reigns with you in the unity of
    the Holy Spirit,
in the splendour of eternal light,
God for ever and ever.

YEAR C

OPEN the heavens,
   almighty Father,
and pour out your Spirit
upon your people gathered in prayer.

Renew the power of our baptismal cleansing
and fill us with zeal for good deeds.
Let us hear your voice once again,
that we may recognize in your beloved Son
our hope of inheriting eternal life.

Grant this through Jesus Christ, your Word
    made flesh,
who lives and reigns with you in the unity of
    the Holy Spirit,
in the splendour of eternal light,
God for ever and ever.

SEASON OF LENT

FIRST SUNDAY OF LENT

LORD our God,
in every age you call a people
to hear your word
and to do your will.

Renew us in these Lenten days:
washed clean of sin,
sealed with the Spirit,
and sustained by your living bread,
may we remain true to our calling
and, with the elect, serve you alone.

Grant this through Christ, our liberator from
sin,
who lives and reigns with you in the unity of
the Holy Spirit,
holy and mighty God for ever and ever.

GOD of the covenant,
as the forty days of deluge
swept away the world's corruption
and watered new beginnings
of righteousness and life,
so in the saving flood of baptism
your people are washed clean and born again.

Lent 1

Throughout these forty days, we beg you,
unseal for us the wellspring of your grace,
cleanse our hearts of all that is not holy,
and cause your gift of new life to flourish once
again.

Grant this through Christ, our liberator from
sin,
who lives and reigns with you in the unity of
the Holy Spirit,
holy and mighty God for ever and ever.

YEAR C LORD our God,
you alone do we worship,
only your word gives life.
Sustain your Church on its Lenten journey.

When we walk through the desert of
temptation,
strengthen us to renounce the power of evil.
When our faith is tested by doubt,
illumine our hearts with Easter's bright
promise.

We ask this through Christ, our deliverance
and hope,
who lives and reigns with you in the unity of
the Holy Spirit,
holy and mighty God for ever and ever.

SECOND SUNDAY OF LENT

YEAR A

HOLY God,
from the dazzling cloud
you revealed Jesus in glory
as your beloved Son.

During these forty days
enlighten your Church with the bright glory of
your presence.
Inspire us by your word,
and so transform us into the image of the risen
Lord,
who lives and reigns with you in the unity of
the Holy Spirit,
holy and mighty God for ever and ever.

YEAR B

EVER-FAITHFUL God,
you were well pleased with Abraham's
obedience
and you accepted the sacrifice of your Son,
who gave himself up for the sake of us all.

Train us by Christ's teaching
and school us in his obedience,
that as we walk his way of sacrifice
we may come to share in your glory.

We ask this through Christ, our deliverance
and hope,
who lives and reigns with you in the unity of
the Holy Spirit,
holy and mighty God for ever and ever.

Lent 2

GOD of the covenant,
your presence fills us with awe,
your word gives us unshakable hope.

Fix in our hearts
the image of your Son in glory,
that, sustained on the path of discipleship,
we may pass over with him to newness of life.

Grant this through Christ, our deliverance and
hope,
who lives and reigns with you in the unity of
the Holy Spirit,
holy and mighty God for ever and ever.

THIRD SUNDAY OF LENT

YEAR A

O God, living and true,
   look upon your people,
whose dry and stony hearts are parched with
   thirst.

Unseal the living water of your Spirit;
let it become within us an ever-flowing spring,
leaping up to eternal life.
Thus may we worship you in spirit and in
   truth
through Christ, our deliverance and hope,
who lives and reigns with you in the unity of
   the Holy Spirit,
holy and mighty God for ever and ever.

YEAR B

HOLY God,
   the folly of the cross
mocks our human wisdom,
and the weakness of the crucified
puts worldly power to shame.

Banish from our hearts
every pretence of might and of knowledge,
that by the power flowing from Christ's
   resurrection
your people may be raised up from the death
   of sin
and fashioned into a living temple of your
   glory.

Grant this through Christ, our liberator from
   sin,
who lives and reigns with you in the unity of
   the Holy Spirit,
holy and mighty God for ever and ever.

YEAR C GOD of salvation,
      we stand before you on holy ground,
for your name is glorified
and your mercy revealed
wherever your mighty deeds are remembered.

Since you are holy and forbearing,
turn us from every rash and shallow judgment
to seek the ways of repentance.

We ask this through Christ, our deliverance
   and hope,
who lives and reigns with you in the unity of
   the Holy Spirit,
holy and mighty God for ever and ever.

FOURTH SUNDAY OF LENT

YEAR A

GOD our Creator,
show forth your mighty works
in the midst of your people.

Enlighten your Church,
that we may know your Son
as the true light of the world
and through our worship confess him
as Christ and Lord,
who lives and reigns with you in the unity of
the Holy Spirit,
holy and mighty God for ever and ever.

YEAR B

O God, rich in mercy,
you so loved the world
that when we were dead in our sins,
you sent your only Son for our deliverance.

Lifted up from the earth,
he is light and life;
exalted upon the cross,
he is truth and salvation.

Raise us up with Christ
and make us rich in good works,
that we may walk as children of light
toward the paschal feast of heaven.

We ask this through Christ, our deliverance
and hope,
who lives and reigns with you in the unity of
the Holy Spirit,
holy and mighty God for ever and ever.

YEAR C

GOD of compassion,
you await the sinner's return
and spread a feast to welcome home the lost.

Save us from the temptations
that lead away from you,
and draw us back by the constancy of your
love,
that we may take our place in your household
and gladly share our inheritance with others.

Grant this through Christ, our liberator from
sin,
who lives and reigns with you in the unity of
the Holy Spirit,
holy and mighty God for ever and ever.

FIFTH SUNDAY OF LENT

YEAR A

MERCIFUL God,
you showed your glory to our fallen
race
by sending your Son
to confound the powers of death.

Call us forth from sin's dark tomb.
Break the bonds which hold us,
that we may believe and proclaim Christ,
the cause of our freedom
and the source of life,
who lives and reigns with you in the unity of
the Holy Spirit,
holy and mighty God for ever and ever.

YEAR B

IN our hearts, O God,
you have written a covenant of grace,
sealed by the obedience of Jesus your Son.

Raise us up with Christ,
the grain fallen to earth
that yields a harvest of everlasting life.
Bring us to glorify your name
by following faithfully where he has led.

We ask this through Christ, our deliverance
and hope,
who lives and reigns with you in the unity of
the Holy Spirit,
holy and mighty God for ever and ever.

G OD of power,
  God of mercy,
you bring forth springs in the wasteland
and turn despair into hope.

Look not upon the sins of our past,
but lift from our hearts
the failures that weigh us down,
that we may find refreshment and life
in Christ, our liberator from sin,
who lives and reigns with you in the unity of
  the Holy Spirit,
holy and mighty God for ever and ever.

HOLY WEEK

PASSION SUNDAY

(Palm Sunday)

O God of eternal glory,
    you anointed Jesus your servant
to bear our sins,
to encourage the weary,
to raise up and restore the fallen.

Keep before our eyes
the splendour of the paschal mystery of Christ,
and, by our sharing in the passion and
    resurrection,
seal our lives with the victorious sign
of his obedience and exaltation.

We ask this through Christ, our liberator from
    sin,
who lives with you in the unity of the Holy
    Spirit,
holy and mighty God for ever and ever.

THE CHRISM MASS

LORD God of our salvation,
you anointed Jesus with the Holy Spirit
to proclaim joyful news to the brokenhearted
and healing for the afflicted.

As we complete this season of conversion,
anoint our hearts with the oil of gladness,
that we may rejoice
in the great feast of our salvation.

We ask this through our Lord Jesus Christ,
your Son,
who lives and reigns with you in the unity of
the Holy Spirit,
God for ever and ever.

HOLY THURSDAY

Evening Mass of the Lord's Supper

O God,
in the fullness of time you revealed your
love
in Jesus the Lord.
On the eve of his death,
as a sign of your covenant,
he washed the feet of his disciples
and gave himself as food and drink.

Give us life at this sacred banquet
and joy in humble service,
that, bound to Christ in all things,
we may pass over from this world to your
kingdom,
where he lives with you now and always in the
unity of the Holy Spirit,
God for ever and ever.

GOOD FRIDAY

Celebration of the Lord's Passion

FROM the throne of grace, O God of
  mercy,
at the hour your Son gave himself to death,
hear the devout prayer of your people.

As he is lifted high upon the cross,
draw into his exalted life
all who are reborn
in the blood and water flowing from his
  opened side.

We ask this through Jesus Christ, our passover
  and our peace,
who lives with you now and always in the
  unity of the Holy Spirit,
God for ever and ever.

SEASON OF EASTER

EASTER SUNDAY

The Resurrection of the Lord

EASTER VIGIL

O God,
your saving plan has brought us
to the glory of this night.
Slaves, we become your sons and daughters,
poor, your mercy makes us rich,
sinners, you count us among your saints.

Bring us to know the place that is ours
in the unfolding story of your purpose,
and instil in our hearts
the wonder of your salvation.

Grant this through Jesus Christ, our passover
and our peace,
who lives with you now and always in the
unity of the Holy Spirit,
God for ever and ever.

Easter Day

G OD of undying life,
     by your mighty hand
you raised up Jesus from the grave
and appointed him judge of the living and the
     dead.

Bestow upon those baptized into his death
the power flowing from his resurrection,
that we may proclaim near and far
the pardon and peace you give us.

Grant this through our Lord Jesus Christ,
     first-born from the dead,
who lives with you now and always in the
     unity of the Holy Spirit,
God for ever and ever.

Opening Prayers

When the gospel from Luke 24:13–35 is read

O God, worker of wonders,
  you made this day for joy and gladness.

Let the risen Lord abide with us this evening,
opening the Scriptures to us
and breaking bread in our midst.

Set our hearts aflame and open our eyes,
that we may see in his sufferings
all that the prophets spoke
and recognize him at this table,
the Christ now entered into glory, first-born
    from the dead,
who lives with you now and always in the
    unity of the Holy Spirit,
God for ever and ever.

SECOND SUNDAY OF EASTER

G OD of life,
 source of all faith,
through the waters of baptism
you have raised us up in Jesus
and given us life that endures.

Day by day refine our faith,
that we who have not seen the Christ
may truly confess him as our Lord and God,
and share the blessedness of those who believe.

Grant this through Jesus Christ, the
 resurrection and the life,
who lives and reigns with you in the unity of
 the Holy Spirit,
God for ever and ever.

THIRD SUNDAY OF EASTER

YEAR A

O God of mystery,
   out of death you delivered Christ Jesus,
and he walked in hidden glory with his
   disciples.

Stir up our faith,
that our hearts may burn within us
at the sound of his word,
and our eyes be opened to recognize him
in the breaking of the bread.

Grant this through Jesus Christ, the first-born
   from the dead,
who lives and reigns with you in the unity of
   the Holy Spirit,
God for ever and ever.

YEAR B

G OD of all the prophets,
   you fulfilled your promise of old
that your Christ would suffer
and so rise to glory.

Open our minds to understand the Scriptures
and fill us with joyful wonder in the presence
   of the risen Christ,
that we may be his witnesses
to the farthest reaches of the earth.

We ask this through Jesus Christ, the first-born
    from the dead,
who lives and reigns with you in the unity of
    the Holy Spirit,
God for ever and ever.

YEAR C   G OD of life,
       in your risen Son
you reveal your abiding presence among us
and summon those reborn in baptism
to lives of worship and service.

Fill this assembly with reverence
as we come before you in prayer.
Grant us courage and zeal
in bearing witness before the world
to your Son, Jesus Christ, the first-born from
    the dead,
who lives and reigns with you in the unity of
    the Holy Spirit,
God for ever and ever.

FOURTH SUNDAY OF EASTER

YEAR A

O God,
 you never cease to call even those far
 away,
for it is your will
that all be drawn into one fold.

Attune our ears to the voice of the Good
 Shepherd,
who leads us always to you,
that we may find under your tender protection
life in all its fullness.

We ask this through Jesus Christ, the
 resurrection and the life,
who lives and reigns with you in the unity of
 the Holy Spirit,
God for ever and ever.

YEAR B

GOD of lasting love,
 fulfil your plan of salvation
to gather into one fold
the peoples of the whole world.

Let everyone on earth
recognize your Christ as the Good Shepherd,
who freely lays down his life for all
to take it up again in power.

Grant this through Jesus Christ, the
   resurrection and the life,
who lives and reigns with you in the unity of
   the Holy Spirit,
God for ever and ever.

YEAR C   SAFE in your hand, O God,
      is the flock you shepherd
through Jesus your Son.

Lead us always to the living waters
where you promise respite and refreshment,
that we may be counted among those
who know and follow you.

We ask this through Jesus Christ, the
   resurrection and the life,
who lives and reigns with you in the unity of
   the Holy Spirit,
God for ever and ever.

FIFTH SUNDAY OF EASTER

YEAR A

WE have beheld your glory, O God,
in the face of Christ Jesus your Son.

Enliven our faith,
that through Christ we may put our trust in
you.
Deepen our faith,
that in Christ we may serve you.
Complete our faith,
that one day we may live with you
in that place which Christ prepares for us,
where he lives with you in the unity of the
Holy Spirit,
God for ever and ever.

YEAR B

O God,
you graft us on to Christ, the true vine,
and, with tireless care,
you nurture our growth in knowledge and
reverence.

Tend the vineyard of your Church,
that in Christ each branch may bring forth
to the glory of your name
abundant fruits of faith and love.

Grant this through Jesus Christ, the
resurrection and the life,
who lives and reigns with you in the unity of
the Holy Spirit,
God for ever and ever.

YEAR C WE behold your glory, O God,
in the love shown by your Son,
lifted up on the cross
and exalted on high.

Increase our love for one another,
that both in name and in truth
we may be disciples of the risen Lord Jesus,
and so reflect by our lives
the glory that is yours.

Grant this through Jesus Christ, the first-born
from the dead,
who lives and reigns with you in the unity of
the Holy Spirit,
God for ever and ever.

SIXTH SUNDAY OF EASTER

YEAR A

FAITHFUL God,
who loves us in Christ Jesus,
send your Spirit of truth to dwell within us,
that we may always reject what is false,
live by the commands of Christ,
and be true to the love you have shown us.

Grant this through Jesus Christ, the
resurrection and the life,
who lives and reigns with you in the unity of
the Holy Spirit,
God for ever and ever.

YEAR B

GOD of all nations,
in the gift of your Son
you have embraced the world
with a love that takes away our sin
and bestows perfect joy.

Grant to all who have been reborn in baptism
fidelity in serving you
and generosity in loving one another.

We ask this through Jesus Christ, the first-born
from the dead,
who lives and reigns with you in the unity of
the Holy Spirit,
God for ever and ever.

YEAR C

GREAT and loving Father,
your will for us in Jesus
is the peace the world cannot give;
your abiding gift
is the Advocate he promised.

Calm all troubled hearts,
dispel every fear.
Keep us steadfast in love
and faithful to your word,
that we may always be your dwelling place.

Grant this through Jesus Christ, the first-born
from the dead,
who lives and reigns with you in the unity of
the Holy Spirit,
God for ever and ever.

THE ASCENSION OF THE LORD

YEAR A

GOD of majesty,
 yours is the power that raised Christ
 from death,
yours the glory that exalted him to your right
 hand.

By the mystery of the Ascension,
sustain our hope
as we bear witness to our baptism.
By the perpetual outpouring of your Spirit,
confirm your Church
in its mission of salvation.

Grant this through Jesus Christ, the first-born
 from the dead,
who lives and reigns with you in the unity of
 the Holy Spirit,
God for ever and ever.

YEAR B

GOD of power and might,
 in the mystery of the Ascension
you have raised up and glorified your Son,
and exalted our humanity at your right hand.

Confirm the good news your Church
 proclaims,
so that when Christ returns in glory
all nations may be gathered into the kingdom,
where he lives and reigns with you in the unity
 of the Holy Spirit,
God for ever and ever.

The Ascension

GOD of majesty,
you led the Messiah
through suffering into risen life
and took him up to the glory of heaven.

Clothe us with the power
promised from on high,
and send us forth to the ends of the earth
as heralds of repentance
and witnesses of Jesus Christ, the first-born
from the dead,
who lives and reigns with you in the unity of
the Holy Spirit,
God for ever and ever.

SEVENTH SUNDAY OF EASTER

YEAR A

GOD our Father,
glorify your Son
in the lives of the people called by his name.
Through no merit of ours, you have made us
    your own,
to be your witnesses on earth.
Keep us true to the name we bear,
that people everywhere may know
that you are the God and lover of us all.

We ask this through Jesus Christ, the
    resurrection and the life,
who lives and reigns with you in the unity of
    the Holy Spirit,
God for ever and ever.

YEAR B

FATHER most holy,
look upon this people
whom you have sanctified by the dying and
    rising of your Son.
Keep us one in love
and consecrate us in your truth,
that the new life you have given us
may bring us to the fullness of joy.

Grant this through Jesus Christ, the first-born
    from the dead,
who lives and reigns with you in the unity of
    the Holy Spirit,
God for ever and ever.

Easter 7

FATHER, righteous one,
  your beloved Son prayed
that his disciples in every generation
might be one as you and he are one.

Look upon this assembly
gathered in his name.
Fulfil in us the prayer of Jesus
and crown our celebration of this paschal
    season
with your Spirit's gift of unity and love.

Grant this through Jesus Christ, the first-born
    from the dead,
who lives and reigns with you in the unity of
    the Holy Spirit,
God for ever and ever.

PENTECOST SUNDAY

VIGIL MASS

GOD of majesty and glory,
you bring us to the day
that crowns our joyful Easter feast.

Open for us the fountain of living waters
promised to the faithful,
that the outpouring of the Spirit
may reveal Christ's glory
and enlighten all who wait in hope
for the glorious day of redemption.

We ask this through Jesus Christ, the
resurrection and the life,
who lives and reigns with you in the unity of
the Holy Spirit,
God for ever and ever.

MASS DURING THE DAY

SEND down, O God, upon your people
the flame of your Holy Spirit,
and fill with the abundance of your sevenfold
    gift
the Church you brought forth
from your Son's pierced side.

May your life-giving Spirit
lend fire to our words
and strength to our witness.
Send us forth to the nations of the world
to proclaim with boldness your wondrous
    work
of raising Christ to your right hand.

We make our prayer through our Lord Jesus
    Christ, your Son,
who lives and reigns with you in the unity of
    the Holy Spirit,
God for ever and ever.

THE HOLY TRINITY

Sunday after Pentecost

YEAR A

MERCIFUL and gracious Father,
you showed the fullness of your love
when you gave your only Son for our salvation
and sent down upon us the power of your
    Spirit.

Complete within us the work of your love,
that we who have communion in Christ
may come to share fully
the undying life he lives with you,
in the unity of the Holy Spirit,
God for ever and ever.

YEAR B

GOD our Father,
you have given us a share
in the life that is yours
with your Son and the Holy Spirit.

Strengthen that life within your Church,
that we may know your presence,
observe your commands,
and proclaim the gospel to every nation.

We ask this through our Lord Jesus Christ,
    your Son,
who lives and reigns with you in the unity of
    the Holy Spirit,
God for ever and ever.

YEAR C

O God,
your name is veiled in mystery,
yet we dare to call you Father;
your Son was begotten before all ages,
yet is born among us in time;
your Holy Spirit fills the whole creation,
yet is poured forth now into our hearts.

Because you have made us and loved us
and called us by name,
draw us more deeply into your divine life,
that we may glorify you rightly, through your
    Son,
in the unity of the Holy Spirit,
God for ever and ever.

THE BODY AND BLOOD OF CHRIST

Thursday or Sunday after The Holy Trinity

YEAR A

THE bread you give, O God,
   is Christ's flesh for the life of the world;
the cup of his blood
is your covenant for our salvation.

Grant that we who worship Christ in this holy
      mystery
may reverence him in the needy of this world
by lives poured out for the sake of that
      kingdom
where he lives and reigns with you in the unity
   of the Holy Spirit,
God for ever and ever.

YEAR B

GOD ever faithful,
   you have made a covenant with your
      people
in the gift of your Son,
who offered his body for us
and poured out his blood for the many.

As we celebrate this eucharistic sacrifice,
build up your Church
by deepening within us the life of your
      covenant
and by opening our hearts to those in need.

The Body and Blood of Christ

We ask this through our Lord Jesus Christ,
    your Son,
who lives and reigns with you in the unity of
    the Holy Spirit,
God for ever and ever.

YEAR C YOU have blessed all generations,
    O God most high,
in Jesus, our compassionate Saviour,
for through him you invite us to your
    kingdom,
welcome us to your table,
and provide us with nourishment in
    abundance.

Teach us to imitate your unfailing kindness
and to build up Christ's body, the Church,
by generously handing on to others
the gifts we have received from your bounty.

We ask this through our Lord Jesus Christ,
    your Son,
who lives and reigns with you in the unity of
    the Holy Spirit,
God for ever and ever.

THE SACRED HEART OF JESUS

Friday following Second Sunday after Pentecost

YEAR A

G OD of love,
you set your heart upon the least of nations,
and in the heart of Jesus
you reveal your love to the merest of children.

Make us simple enough to receive your great love,
and strong enough to bear it to others.

Grant this through our Lord Jesus Christ, your Son,
who lives and reigns with you in the unity of the Holy Spirit,
God for ever and ever.

YEAR B

G OD of life and love,
from the pierced heart of your Son
flowed water and blood,
cleansing the world
and giving birth to your Church.

Renew within your people
the love poured out on us in baptism,
and through the blessing-cup we share
keep us always faithful
to your life-giving covenant.

The Sacred Heart of Jesus

We make our prayer through our Lord Jesus
    Christ, your Son,
who lives and reigns with you in the unity of
    the Holy Spirit,
God for ever and ever.

YEAR C

ETERNAL God,
    in Christ you have sought us
with a shepherd's heart,
and we have rejoiced
to be found and restored.

Multiply in all the world
the wonders of your saving grace,
and gather your scattered people
until heaven resounds in jubilation
at humanity made whole
and creation restored.

We ask this through our Lord Jesus Christ,
    your Son,
who lives and reigns with you in the unity of
    the Holy Spirit,
God for ever and ever.

ORDINARY TIME

SECOND SUNDAY IN ORDINARY TIME

(The Sunday between 14 & 20 January inclusive)

YEAR A   MERCIFUL God,
you sent your Son, the spotless Lamb,
to take upon himself the sin of the world.

Make our lives holy,
that your Church may bear witness to your
    purpose
of reconciling all things in Christ,
who lives and reigns with you in the unity of
    the Holy Spirit,
God for ever and ever.

YEAR B   FROM our earliest days, O God,
you call us by name.

Make our ears attentive to your voice,
our spirits eager to respond,
that, having heard you in Jesus your anointed
    one,
we may draw others to be his disciples.

We ask this through our Lord Jesus Christ,
    your Son,
who lives and reigns with you in the unity of
    the Holy Spirit,
God for ever and ever.

GOD of wonders,
at Cana in Galilee
you revealed your glory in Jesus Christ
and summoned all humanity
to life in him.

Show to your people gathered on this day
your transforming power
and give us a foretaste
of the wine you keep
for the age to come.

We make our prayer through our Lord Jesus
Christ, your Son,
who lives and reigns with you in the unity of
the Holy Spirit,
God for ever and ever.

THIRD SUNDAY IN ORDINARY TIME

(The Sunday between 21 & 27 January inclusive)

YEAR A

GOD of salvation,
the splendour of your glory
dispels the darkness of earth,
for in Christ we behold
the nearness of your kingdom.

Now make us quick to follow where he
beckons,
eager to embrace the tasks of the gospel.

We ask this through our Lord Jesus Christ,
your Son,
who lives and reigns with you in the unity of
the Holy Spirit,
God for ever and ever.

YEAR B

YOUR sovereign rule, O God,
draws near to us
in the person of Jesus your Son.
Your word summons us to faith;
your power transforms our lives.

Free us to follow in Christ's footsteps,
so that neither human loyalty
nor earthly attachment
may hold us back from answering your call.

We ask this through our Lord Jesus Christ,
    your Son,
who lives and reigns with you in the unity of
    the Holy Spirit,
God for ever and ever.

YEAR C   L ORD God,
          whose compassion embraces all peoples,
whose law is wisdom, freedom, and joy for the
    poor,
fulfil in our midst your promise of favour,
that we may receive the gospel of salvation
    with faith
and, anointed by the Spirit, freely proclaim it.

Grant this through our Lord Jesus Christ, your
    Son,
who lives and reigns with you in the unity of
    the Holy Spirit,
God for ever and ever.

FOURTH SUNDAY IN ORDINARY TIME

(The Sunday between 28 January & 3 February inclusive)

YEAR A

O God,
    teach us the hidden wisdom of the gospel,
so that we may hunger and thirst for holiness,
work tirelessly for peace,
and be counted among those
who seek first the blessedness of your
    kingdom.

We ask this through our Lord Jesus Christ,
    your Son,
who lives and reigns with you in the unity of
    the Holy Spirit,
God for ever and ever.

YEAR B

FAITHFUL God,
    your Holy One, Jesus of Nazareth,
spoke the truth with authority,
and you confirmed his teaching by wondrous
    deeds.

Through his healing presence,
drive far from us all that is unholy,
so that by word and deed
we may proclaim him Messiah and Lord
and bear witness to your power to heal and
    save.

We ask this through our Lord Jesus Christ,
 your Son,
who lives and reigns with you in the unity of
 the Holy Spirit,
God for ever and ever.

YEAR C GOD of salvation,
  in your Prophet, Jesus the Christ,
you announce freedom
and summon us to conversion.

As we marvel at the grace and power of your
 word,
enlighten us to see the beauty of the gospel
and strengthen us to embrace its demands.

Grant this through our Lord Jesus Christ, your
 Son,
who lives and reigns with you in the unity of
 the Holy Spirit,
God for ever and ever.

*The above is replaced if the Feast of the Presentation of
the Lord is celebrated on this Sunday*

FIFTH SUNDAY IN ORDINARY TIME

(The Sunday between 4 & 10 February inclusive, if before Lent)

YEAR A

HEAVENLY Father,
you have called your Church
to be the salt of the earth and the light of the
world.

Give us vigorous faith and a love that is
genuine,
so that all may see our works
and give you the glory.

We make our prayer through our Lord Jesus
Christ, your Son,
who lives and reigns with you in the unity of
the Holy Spirit,
God for ever and ever.

YEAR B

OUT of your power and compassion,
O God,
you sent your Son into our afflicted world
to proclaim the day of salvation.

Heal the brokenhearted;
bind up our wounds.
Bring us health of body and spirit
and raise us to new life in your service.

We make our prayer through our Lord Jesus
Christ, your Son,

who lives and reigns with you in the unity of
the Holy Spirit,
God for ever and ever.

YEAR C

MOST holy God,
the earth is filled with your glory,
and in your presence angels stand in awe.

Enlarge our vision,
that we may recognize your power at work in
your Son
and join the apostles and prophets
as heralds of your saving word.

We ask this through our Lord Jesus Christ,
your Son,
who lives and reigns with you in the unity of
the Holy Spirit,
God for ever and ever.

SIXTH SUNDAY IN ORDINARY TIME

(The Sunday between 11 & 17 February inclusive, if before Lent, or the Sunday between 8 & 14 May inclusive, if after the Sunday after Pentecost – The Holy Trinity)

YEAR A

ALL-SEEING God,
you alone judge rightly our inmost thoughts.

Teach us to observe your law from the heart
even as we keep it outwardly.
Purify our desires,
calm every anger,
and reconcile us to one another.
Then will our worship at your altar
render you perfect praise.

We make our prayer through our Lord Jesus Christ, your Son,
who lives and reigns with you in the unity of the Holy Spirit,
God for ever and ever.

YEAR B

WE come before you, O God,
confident in Christ's victory over sickness and death.

Heal us again
from sin, which divides us,

and from prejudice, which isolates us.
Bring us to wholeness of life
through the pardon you grant your people.

We ask this through our Lord Jesus Christ,
    your Son,
who lives and reigns with you in the unity of
    the Holy Spirit,
God for ever and ever.

YEAR C

O God,
    who alone can satisfy our deepest
    hungers,
protect us from the lure of wealth and power;
move our hearts to seek first your kingdom,
that ours may be the security and joy
of those who place their trust in you.

We make our prayer through our Lord Jesus
    Christ, your Son,
who lives and reigns with you in the unity of
    the Holy Spirit,
God for ever and ever.

SEVENTH SUNDAY IN ORDINARY TIME

(The Sunday between 18 & 24 February inclusive, if before Lent, or the Sunday between 15 & 21 May, if after the Sunday after Pentecost – The Holy Trinity)

YEAR A

HEAVENLY Father,
in Christ Jesus
you challenge us to renounce violence
and to forsake revenge.

Teach us to recognize as your children
even our enemies and persecutors
and to love them without measure or
    discrimination.

We ask this through our Lord Jesus Christ,
    your Son,
who lives and reigns with you in the unity of
    the Holy Spirit,
God for ever and ever.

YEAR B

GOD of pardon and deliverance,
your forgiving love, revealed in Christ,
has brought to birth a new creation.

Raise us up from our sins
to walk in your ways,
that we may witness to your power,
which makes all things new.

Grant this through our Lord Jesus Christ, your
    Son,

who lives and reigns with you in the unity of
    the Holy Spirit,
God for ever and ever.

YEAR C   COMPASSIONATE God and Father,
       you are kind to the ungrateful,
merciful even to the wicked.

Pour out your love upon us,
that with good and generous hearts
we may keep from judging others
and learn your way of compassion.

We make our prayer through our Lord Jesus
    Christ, your Son,
who lives and reigns with you in the unity of
    the Holy Spirit,
God for ever and ever.

EIGHTH SUNDAY IN ORDINARY TIME

(The Sunday between 17 & 25 February inclusive, if before Lent, or the Sunday between 22 & 28 May, if after the Sunday after Pentecost – The Holy Trinity)

YEAR A

L ORD God,
your care for us surpasses
even a mother's tender love.

Through this word and sacrament
renew our trust in your provident care,
that we may abandon all anxiety
and seek first your kingdom.

We make our prayer through our Lord Jesus
Christ, your Son,
who lives and reigns with you in the unity of
the Holy Spirit,
God for ever and ever.

YEAR B

G OD of tenderness,
desire of the human heart,
you led your people into the desert
and made them your own in love and fidelity.

By this word and sacrament
renew with us your covenant of love,
so that, forsaking the ways of the past,
we may embrace the new life of the kingdom.

We make our prayer through our Lord Jesus
Christ, your Son,

who lives and reigns with you in the unity of
   the Holy Spirit,
God for ever and ever.

YEAR C   O God, our teacher and judge,
        hear our prayer
as we gather at the table of your word.

Enrich our hearts with the goodness of your
   wisdom
and renew us from within,
that all our actions, all our words,
may bear the fruit of your transforming grace.

We make our prayer through our Lord Jesus
   Christ, your Son,
who lives and reigns with you in the unity of
   the Holy Spirit,
God for ever and ever.

NINTH SUNDAY IN ORDINARY TIME

(The Sunday between 24 February and 2 March inclusive, if before Lent, or the Sunday between 29 May & 4 June, if after the Sunday after Pentecost – The Holy Trinity)

YEAR A

GOD of justice,
rock of our salvation,
open our minds and hearts to Jesus your Son.

Let us hold fast to his words
and express them in deeds,
that our faith may be built on a sure
    foundation
and our lives be judged worthy of you.

Grant this through our Lord Jesus Christ, your
    Son,
who lives and reigns with you in the unity of
    the Holy Spirit,
God for ever and ever.

YEAR B

HOLY God,
you sanctified this day
as a time for rest and worship.

As its blessed hours unfold,
place on our lips canticles of praise
and in our hearts the charity of Christ,
that this day may be a pledge and foretaste
of the eternal kingdom yet to come.

We ask this through our Lord Jesus Christ,
    your Son,
who lives and reigns with you in the unity of
    the Holy Spirit,
God for ever and ever.

YEAR C

GOD of the nations,
    whose will it is that all be saved
and come to knowledge of the truth,
grant that your gift of faith
may be alive in every heart,
so that, unworthy as we are,
we may welcome your Son
and find healing in his word.

We ask this through our Lord Jesus Christ,
    your Son,
who lives and reigns with you in the unity of
    the Holy Spirit,
God for ever and ever.

TENTH SUNDAY IN ORDINARY TIME

(The Sunday between 5 & 11 June inclusive, or if after the Sunday after Pentecost – The Holy Trinity)

YEAR A

O God,
    whose judgment shines like the light of day,
you invite sinners and outcasts
to the banquet of salvation.

Heal our pride and self-righteousness
as you send down upon us
the gentle rain of your mercy.

We make our prayer through our Lord Jesus Christ, your Son,
who lives and reigns with you in the unity of the Holy Spirit,
God for ever and ever.

YEAR B

GOD our redeemer,
    in Jesus, your promised Messiah,
you crushed the power of Satan.

Sustain your Church in the struggle against evil,
that, hearing your word and doing your will,
we may be fashioned into a household of true disciples
who share in the victory of the cross.

Grant this through our Lord Jesus Christ, your
    Son,
who lives and reigns with you in the unity of
    the Holy Spirit,
God for ever and ever.

YEAR C

O God,
    our very breath, our only hope,
in every age you take pity on us
and bring forth life from death.

Visit your people
and raise your Church to new life,
that we may join with all generations
in voicing our wonder and praise.

We make our prayer through our Lord Jesus
    Christ, your Son,
who lives and reigns with you in the unity of
    the Holy Spirit,
God for ever and ever.

ELEVENTH SUNDAY IN ORDINARY TIME

(The Sunday between 12 & 18 June inclusive)

YEAR A

COMPASSIONATE God,
your word calls labourers to the harvest.

Send us who are blest with the gift of your
kingdom
to announce its coming with gladness
and to manifest its healing power.

We make our prayer through our Lord Jesus
Christ, your Son,
who lives and reigns with you in the unity of
the Holy Spirit,
God for ever and ever.

YEAR B

O God,
at whose bidding the seed will sprout
and the shoot grow towards full stature,
hear the prayer of your assembled people.

Make us trust in your hidden ways,
that we may pray with confidence
and wait for your kingdom now growing in
our midst.

We ask this through our Lord Jesus Christ,
your Son,
who lives and reigns with you in the unity of
the Holy Spirit,
God for ever and ever.

YEAR C

COMPASSIONATE God,
you gather your people in prayer
and lavish your gifts upon us anew.

Sinners that we are,
you have forgiven us much.
Grant that our experience of your pardon
may increase our love
until it reflects your own immeasurable
forgiveness.

We make our prayer through our Lord Jesus
Christ, your Son,
who lives and reigns with you in the unity of
the Holy Spirit,
God for ever and ever.

TWELFTH SUNDAY IN ORDINARY TIME

(The Sunday between 19 & 25 June inclusive)

YEAR A TRUE and faithful God,
you give courage to the fearful
and endurance to martyrs.

Sustain us as followers of your Son Jesus,
that with boldness and conviction
we may acknowledge him before the world.

We ask this through our Lord Jesus Christ,
your Son,
who lives and reigns with you in the unity of
the Holy Spirit,
God for ever and ever.

YEAR B IN the beginning, O God,
your word subdued the chaos;
in the fullness of time
you sent Jesus, your Son,
to rebuke the forces of evil
and bring forth a new creation.

By that same power,
transform all our fear
into faith and awe in your saving presence.

We ask this through our Lord Jesus Christ,
your Son,
who lives and reigns with you in the unity of
the Holy Spirit,
God for ever and ever.

YEAR C

O God,
whose Son, our Messiah and Lord,
did not turn aside from the path of suffering
nor spare his disciples the prospect of
    rejection,
pour out your Spirit upon this assembly,
that we may abandon the security of the easy
    way
and follow in Christ's footsteps
towards the cross and true life.

Grant this through our Lord Jesus Christ, your
    Son,
who lives and reigns with you in the unity of
    the Holy Spirit,
God for ever and ever.

THIRTEENTH SUNDAY IN ORDINARY TIME

(The Sunday between 26 June & 2 July inclusive)

YEAR A

ALL-POWERFUL God,
your incarnate Word commands our
obedience
and offers us true life.

Make our ears attentive to the voice of your
Son
and our hearts generous in answering his call,
that we may take up the cross with trust in his
promises.

We ask this through our Lord Jesus Christ,
your Son,
who lives and reigns with you in the unity of
the Holy Spirit,
God for ever and ever.

YEAR B

GOD of the living,
in whose image we have been formed
with imperishable life as our destiny,
dispel from your people the fear of death
and awaken within us the faith that saves.
Bid us rise from the death of sin
to take our place in the new creation.

We make our prayer through our Lord Jesus
Christ, your Son,

who lives and reigns with you in the unity of
the Holy Spirit,
God for ever and ever.

YEAR C SOVEREIGN God, ruler of our hearts,
you call us to obedience
and sustain us in freedom.

Keep us true to the way of your Son,
that we may leave behind all that hinders us
and, with eyes fixed on him,
walk surely in the path of the kingdom.

Grant this through our Lord Jesus Christ, your
Son,
who lives and reigns with you in the unity of
the Holy Spirit,
God for ever and ever.

FOURTEENTH SUNDAY IN ORDINARY TIME

(The Sunday between 3 & 9 July inclusive)

YEAR A

FATHER, Lord of heaven and earth,
  by whose gracious will
the mysteries of the kingdom are revealed to
  the childlike,
make us learn from your Son humility of
  heart,
that in shouldering his yoke
we may find refreshment and rest.

We ask this through our Lord Jesus Christ,
  your Son,
who lives and reigns with you in the unity of
  the Holy Spirit,
God for ever and ever.

YEAR B

GOD of the prophets,
  in every age you send the word of truth,
familiar yet new,
a sign of contradiction.

Let us not be counted among those who lack
  faith,
but give us the vision
to see Christ in our midst
and to welcome your saving word.

Grant this through our Lord Jesus Christ, your
    Son,
who lives and reigns with you in the unity of
    the Holy Spirit,
God for ever and ever.

YEAR C   BOUNDLESS, O God, is your saving
       power;
your harvest reaches to the ends of the
    earth.

Fill our hearts with zeal for your kingdom
and place on our lips the tidings of peace.
Grant us perseverance as heralds of the gospel
and joy as disciples of your Son, Jesus Christ
    our Lord,
who lives and reigns with you in the unity of
    the Holy Spirit,
God for ever and ever.

FIFTEENTH SUNDAY IN ORDINARY TIME

(The Sunday between 10 & 16 July inclusive)

YEAR A

GOD of the heavens,
God of the earth,
all creation awaits your gift of new life.

Prepare our hearts
to receive the word of your Son,
that his gospel may grow within us
and yield a harvest that is a hundredfold.

We ask this through our Lord Jesus Christ,
your Son,
who lives and reigns with you in the unity of
the Holy Spirit,
God for ever and ever.

YEAR B

GOD of justice, God of salvation,
from every land you call a people to
yourself.
Yours is the work we do,
yours the message we carry.

Keep your Church single-minded and faithful
to you.
Let failure not discourage us
nor success beguile our hearts,
as you send us to proclaim the gospel.

We make our prayer through our Lord Jesus
    Christ, your Son,
who lives and reigns with you in the unity of
    the Holy Spirit,
God for ever and ever.

YEAR C   IN Christ you draw near to us,
      God of mercy and compassion,
lifting us out of death,
binding up our wounds,
and nursing our spirits back to health.

Let such a tenderness as yours compel us
to go and do likewise.

Grant this through our Lord Jesus Christ, your
    Son,
who lives and reigns with you in the unity of
    the Holy Spirit,
God for ever and ever.

SIXTEENTH SUNDAY IN ORDINARY TIME

(The Sunday between 17 & 23 July inclusive)

YEAR A

O God, patient and forbearing,
    you alone know fully
the goodness of what you have made.

Strengthen our spirit when we are slow
and temper our zeal when we are rash,
that in your own good time
you may produce in us a rich harvest
from the seed you have sown and tended.

We make our prayer through our Lord Jesus
    Christ, your Son,
who lives and reigns with you in the unity of
    the Holy Spirit,
God for ever and ever.

YEAR B

COMPASSIONATE God,
    from far and near you gather your
    Church into one.

Safeguard the unity of your flock
through the teaching of Christ the Shepherd,
that all your scattered children may find in him
the guidance and nourishment they seek.

We ask this through our Lord Jesus Christ,
    your Son,
who lives and reigns with you in the unity of
    the Holy Spirit,
God for ever and ever.

YEAR C

ETERNAL God,
you draw near to us in Christ
and make yourself our guest.

Amid the cares of our daily lives,
make us attentive to your voice
and alert to your presence,
that we may treasure your word above all else.

We ask this through our Lord Jesus Christ,
your Son,
who lives and reigns with you in the unity of
the Holy Spirit,
God for ever and ever.

SEVENTEENTH SUNDAY IN ORDINARY TIME

(The Sunday between 24 & 30 July inclusive)

YEAR A

GOD of eternal wisdom,
you alone impart the gift of right
judgment.

Grant us an understanding heart,
that we may value wisely
the treasure of your kingdom
and gladly forgo all lesser gifts
to possess that kingdom's incomparable joy.

We make our prayer through our Lord Jesus
Christ, your Son,
who lives and reigns with you in the unity of
the Holy Spirit,
God for ever and ever.

YEAR B

O God, you open wide your hand,
giving us food in due season.

Out of your never-failing abundance,
satisfy the hungers of body and soul
and lead all peoples of the earth
to the feast of the world to come.

We make our prayer through our Lord Jesus
Christ, your Son,
who lives and reigns with you in the unity of
the Holy Spirit,
God for ever and ever.

YEAR C PROVIDENT Father,
with the prayer your Son taught us
always on our lips,
we ask, we seek, we knock at your door.

In our every need,
grant us the first and best of all your gifts,
the Spirit who makes us your children.

We ask this through our Lord Jesus Christ,
your Son,
who lives and reigns with you in the unity of
the Holy Spirit,
God for ever and ever.

EIGHTEENTH SUNDAY IN ORDINARY TIME

(The Sunday between 31 July & 6 August inclusive)

YEAR A

BOUNTIFUL and compassionate God,
you place in the hands of your disciples
the food of life.

Nourish us at your holy table,
that we may bear Christ to others
and share with them
the gifts we have so richly received.

We make our prayer through our Lord Jesus
Christ, your Son,
who lives and reigns with you in the unity of
the Holy Spirit,
God for ever and ever.

YEAR B

LORD, giver of lasting life,
satisfy our hunger through Christ, the
Bread of Life,
and quench our thirst with your gift of belief,
that we may no longer work for food that
perishes,
but believe in the One whom you have sent.

We ask this through our Lord Jesus Christ,
your Son,
who lives and reigns with you in the unity of
the Holy Spirit,
God for ever and ever.

YEAR C

O God,
the giver of every gift that endures,
only by your grace can we rightly understand
the wonder of life
and why it is given.

By the word of your Son
challenge our foolishness,
confront our greed,
and shape our lives
to the wisdom of the gospel.

We ask this through our Lord Jesus Christ,
your Son,
who lives and reigns with you in the unity of
the Holy Spirit,
God for ever and ever.

NINETEENTH SUNDAY IN ORDINARY TIME

(The Sunday between 7 & 13 August inclusive)

YEAR A

GOD of all power,
your sovereign word comes to us in
Christ.

When your Church is in danger, make firm our
trust;
when your people falter, steady our faith.
Show us in Jesus your power to save,
that we may always acclaim him as Lord,
who lives and reigns with you in the unity of
the Holy Spirit,
God for ever and ever.

YEAR B

GOD our Father and provider,
whose Son has given his flesh for the life
of the world,
sustain your pilgrim Church on its journey
with the word of life and the bread of heaven.
Draw us nearer to him in whose name we
gather,
that, following his way of sacrificial love,
we may come to the banquet of eternal life.

Grant this through our Lord Jesus Christ, your
Son,
who lives and reigns with you in the unity of
the Holy Spirit,
God for ever and ever.

YEAR C

O God,
on whom our faith rests secure
and whose kingdom we await,
sustain us by word and sacrament
and keep us alert for the coming of the Son of
Man,
that we may welcome him without delay.

We ask this through our Lord Jesus Christ,
your Son,
who lives and reigns with you in the unity of
the Holy Spirit,
God for ever and ever.

TWENTIETH SUNDAY IN ORDINARY TIME

(The Sunday between 14 & 20 August inclusive)

YEAR A

GOD of the nations,
to your table all are invited
and in your family no one is a stranger.

Satisfy the hunger
of those gathered in this house of prayer,
and mercifully extend to all the peoples on
earth
the joy of salvation and faith.

Grant this through our Lord Jesus Christ, your
Son,
who lives and reigns with you in the unity of
the Holy Spirit,
God for ever and ever.

YEAR B

WISE and gracious God,
you spread a table before us
and nourish your people with the word of life
and the bread from heaven.

In our sharing of these holy gifts,
show us our unity in you
and give us a taste of the life to come.

We make our prayer through our Lord Jesus
Christ, your Son,
who lives and reigns with you in the unity of
the Holy Spirit,
God for ever and ever.

Ordinary Time 20

TO set the earth ablaze, O God,
your Son submitted to a baptism unto
death,
and from his cup of suffering
you call the Church to drink.

Keep our eyes fixed on Jesus
and give us strength in time of trial
to run the race that lies before us.

We ask this through our Lord Jesus Christ,
your Son,
who lives and reigns with you in the unity of
the Holy Spirit,
God for ever and ever.

TWENTY-FIRST SUNDAY IN ORDINARY TIME

(The Sunday between 21 & 27 August inclusive)

YEAR A

L IVING God,
   you sent your Son among us
to reveal your wisdom
and make known your ways.

Increase our faith,
that we may confess Jesus as your Son,
take up his work on earth,
and trust his promise to sustain the Church.

We ask this through our Lord Jesus Christ,
   your Son,
who lives and reigns with you in the unity of
   the Holy Spirit,
God for ever and ever.

YEAR B

I N every age, O God,
   you give your people freedom
to walk in faith
or to turn away.

Grant us grace
to remain faithful to your Holy One,
whose words are spirit and life,
Jesus Christ, our Lord,
who lives and reigns with you in the unity of
   the Holy Spirit,
God for ever and ever.

YEAR C

TO the banquet of your kingdom,
O God of the nations,
you have invited people of every race and
tongue.

May all who are called to a place at your table
come, by the narrow way,
to the unending feast of life.

We make our prayer through our Lord Jesus
Christ, your Son,
who lives and reigns with you in the unity of
the Holy Spirit,
God for ever and ever.

TWENTY-SECOND SUNDAY IN ORDINARY TIME

(The Sunday between 28 August & 3 September inclusive)

YEAR A

O God,
whose word burns like a fire within us,
grant us a bold and faithful spirit,
that in your strength we may be unafraid
to speak your word
and follow where you lead.

We make our prayer through our Lord Jesus
Christ, your Son,
who lives and reigns with you in the unity of
the Holy Spirit,
God for ever and ever.

YEAR B

FATHER of light,
giver of every good and perfect gift,
bring to fruition the word of truth
sown in our hearts by your Son,
that we may rightly understand your
commandments,
live your law of love,
and so offer you worship that is pure and
undefiled.

Grant this through our Lord Jesus Christ, your
Son,
who lives and reigns with you in the unity of
the Holy Spirit,
God for ever and ever.

YEAR C

GOD and judge of all,
  you show us that the way to your kingdom
is through humility and service.

Keep us true to the path of justice
and give us the reward promised to those
who make a place for the rejected and the
    poor.

We ask this through our Lord Jesus Christ,
    your Son,
who lives and reigns with you in the unity of
    the Holy Spirit,
God for ever and ever.

TWENTY-THIRD SUNDAY IN ORDINARY TIME

(The Sunday between 4 & 10 September inclusive)

YEAR A

CONFIRM, O God, in unity and truth
the Church you gather in Christ.
Encourage the fervent,
enlighten the doubtful,
and bring back the wayward.
Bind us together in mutual love,
that our prayer in Christ's name
may be pleasing to you.

Grant this through our Lord Jesus Christ, your Son,
who lives and reigns with you in the unity of the Holy Spirit,
God for ever and ever.

YEAR B

GOD of power and compassion,
in Christ you reveal your will
to heal and to save.

Open our ears to your redeeming word
and move our hearts by the strength of your love,
so that our every word and work
may proclaim as Messiah
Jesus the Lord,
who lives and reigns with you in the unity of the Holy Spirit,
God for ever and ever.

YEAR C

GOD of the ages,
you call the Church to keep watch in the
world
and to discern the signs of the times.

Grant us the wisdom which your Spirit
bestows,
that with courage we may proclaim your
prophetic word
and complete the work that you have set
before us.

We make our prayer through our Lord Jesus
Christ, your Son,
who lives and reigns with you in the unity of
the Holy Spirit,
God for ever and ever.

TWENTY-FOURTH SUNDAY IN ORDINARY TIME

(The Sunday between 11 & 17 September inclusive)

YEAR A

O God, most high,
you are slow to anger and rich in
compassion.

Keep alive in us the memory of your mercy,
that our angers may be calmed
and our resentments dispelled.
May we discover the forgiveness
promised to those who forgive
and become a people rich in mercy.

We ask this through our Lord Jesus Christ,
your Son,
who lives and reigns with you in the unity of
the Holy Spirit,
God for ever and ever.

YEAR B

MAKE us one, O God,
in acknowledging Jesus the Christ.
As we proclaim him by our words,
let us follow him in our works;
give us strength to take up the cross
and courage to lose our lives for his sake.

We ask this through our Lord Jesus Christ,
your Son,
who lives and reigns with you in the unity of
the Holy Spirit,
God for ever and ever.

YEAR C

UNDAUNTED you seek the lost, O God,
exultant you bring home the found.

Touch our hearts with grateful wonder
at the tenderness of your forbearing love.
Grant us delight in the mercy that has found
us
and bring all to rejoice at the feast of
forgiveness.

We ask this through our Lord Jesus Christ,
your Son,
who lives and reigns with you in the unity of
the Holy Spirit,
God for ever and ever.

TWENTY-FIFTH SUNDAY IN ORDINARY TIME

(The Sunday between 18 & 24 September inclusive)

YEAR A

GOD most high,
your ways are not our ways,
for your kindness is lavished equally upon all.

Teach us to welcome your mercy towards
others,
even as we hope to receive mercy ourselves.

We ask this through our Lord Jesus Christ,
your Son,
who lives and reigns with you in the unity of
the Holy Spirit,
God for ever and ever.

YEAR B

O God,
protector of the poor and defender of
the just,
in your kingdom the last become first,
the gentle are strong,
and the lowly exalted.

Give us wisdom from above,
that we may find in your servant Jesus
the pattern of true discipleship
and the grace to persevere in following him,
who lives and reigns with you in the unity of
the Holy Spirit,
God for ever and ever.

YEAR C GOD our Saviour,
you call us into your service.

Make us wise and resourceful:
children of the light who continue your work
in this world
with untiring concern for integrity and justice.

We ask this through our Lord Jesus Christ,
your Son,
who lives and reigns with you in the unity of
the Holy Spirit,
God for ever and ever.

TWENTY-SIXTH SUNDAY IN ORDINARY TIME

(The Sunday between 25 September & 1 October inclusive)

YEAR A

O God,
you alone judge rightly
and search the depths of the heart.

Make us swift to do your will
and slow to judge our neighbour,
that we may walk with those
who follow the way of repentance and faith
and so enter your heavenly kingdom.

Grant this through our Lord Jesus Christ, your Son,
who lives and reigns with you in the unity of the Holy Spirit,
God for ever and ever.

YEAR B

POUR out your Spirit, O God, over all the world
to inspire every heart
with knowledge and love of you.
Grant that we who confess Jesus as Lord
may shun whatever is contrary to this faith
and give witness to your love
that has saved us in Christ,
for he lives and reigns with you in the unity of the Holy Spirit,
God for ever and ever.

YEAR C

O God of justice,
hear our cry and save us.
Make us heed your word to the prophets;
rouse us to the demand of the gospel
and impel us to carry it out.

We ask this through our Lord Jesus Christ,
your Son,
who lives and reigns with you in the unity of
the Holy Spirit,
God for ever and ever.

TWENTY-SEVENTH SUNDAY IN ORDINARY TIME

(The Sunday between 2 & 8 October inclusive)

YEAR A

YOURS, O God, is the vineyard and its harvest,
yours the kingdom of justice and peace.
You call your people to tend its growth.

Bless the work entrusted to our hands,
that we may offer you
an abundance of just works,
a rich harvest of peace.

We ask this through our Lord Jesus Christ,
your Son,
who lives and reigns with you in the unity of
the Holy Spirit,
God for ever and ever.

YEAR B

CREATOR God,
in Christ you call man and woman
to the fullness of glory
for which you created them in your image.

Heal our hardened hearts,
renew our obedience to your spoken will,
and conform our lives to your gracious design.

Grant this through our Lord Jesus Christ, your
Son,
who lives and reigns with you in the unity of
the Holy Spirit,
God for ever and ever.

YEAR C

GOD, the rock of our salvation,
whose gifts can never fail,
deepen the faith you have already bestowed
and let its power be seen in your servants.

We make our prayer through our Lord Jesus
Christ, your Son,
who lives and reigns with you in the unity of
the Holy Spirit,
God for ever and ever.

TWENTY-EIGHTH SUNDAY IN ORDINARY TIME

(The Sunday between 9 & 15 October inclusive)

YEAR A

GOD of goodness and kindness,
  you invite all peoples to the banquet
and offer them a feast beyond compare.

Give us your saving grace
to keep unstained the robe of our baptism
until that day when you welcome us
to heaven's joyful table.

We ask this through our Lord Jesus Christ,
    your Son,
who lives and reigns with you in the unity of
    the Holy Spirit,
God for ever and ever.

YEAR B

GOD of wisdom,
  whose word probes the motives of our
    hearts,
with you all things are possible.

Let worldly treasure not keep us from Jesus,
who looks on us with love.
Free us to leave all things and follow him,
who lives and reigns with you in the unity of
    the Holy Spirit,
God for ever and ever.

YEAR C

O God,
   our life, our health, our salvation,
look with mercy on your people.
Stir up in us a saving faith,
that believing, we may be healed,
and being healed, we may worthily give you
   thanks.

We ask this through our Lord Jesus Christ,
   your Son,
who lives and reigns with you in the unity of
   the Holy Spirit,
God for ever and ever.

TWENTY-NINTH SUNDAY IN ORDINARY TIME

(The Sunday between 16 & 22 October inclusive)

YEAR A

O God, whose image we bear
and whose name we carry,
yours is the world and all it contains.

Recall us to our true allegiance,
so that above the powers and rulers of this
world
you alone may claim our fullest loyalty and
love.

We make our prayer through our Lord Jesus
Christ, your Son,
who lives and reigns with you in the unity of
the Holy Spirit,
God for ever and ever.

YEAR B

MOST glorious God,
in Jesus you show us
that your will is to save.

Grant to us your people
the boldness to desire a place in your kingdom,
the courage to drink the cup of suffering,
and the grace to find in service
the glory you promise.

We ask this through our Lord Jesus Christ,
   your Son,
who lives and reigns with you in the unity of
   the Holy Spirit,
God for ever and ever.

YEAR C   LORD, tireless guardian of your people,
     always ready to hear the cries of your
   chosen ones,
teach us to rely, day and night, on your care.

Support our prayer lest we grow weary.
Impel us to seek your enduring justice
and your ever-present help.

Grant this through our Lord Jesus Christ, your
   Son,
who lives and reigns with you in the unity of
   the Holy Spirit,
God for ever and ever.

THIRTIETH SUNDAY IN ORDINARY TIME

(The Sunday between 23 & 29 October inclusive)

YEAR A

YOUR love, O God, is boundless.
    We who were strangers
have been made your children.
We who were defenceless
have been brought into your household.

Keep us mindful of your deeds of mercy,
that we may love you with our whole heart
and love our neighbour as ourselves.

We ask this through our Lord Jesus Christ,
    your Son,
who lives and reigns with you in the unity of
    the Holy Spirit,
God for ever and ever.

YEAR B

HAVE pity on us, God our Saviour.
    Grant us grace and courage to cast off
    our sins
and turn to you for healing.
Show us in Christ the sure path of salvation
and strengthen us to follow gladly
in the way of the gospel.

We ask this through our Lord Jesus Christ,
    your Son,
who lives and reigns with you in the unity of
    the Holy Spirit,
God for ever and ever.

YEAR C

O God,
who alone can probe the depths of the
heart,
you hear the prayer of the humble
and justify the repentant sinner.

As we stand before you,
grant us the gift of humility,
that we may see our own sins clearly
and refrain from judging our neighbour.

We make our prayer through our Lord Jesus
Christ, your Son,
who lives and reigns with you in the unity of
the Holy Spirit,
God for ever and ever.

THIRTY-FIRST SUNDAY IN ORDINARY TIME

*(The Sunday between 30 October &
5 November inclusive. For use when All Saints'
Day is not celebrated on this Sunday)*

YEAR A SOVEREIGN God,
we have no father but you,
no teacher but Christ.

Conform our lives to the faith we profess,
preserve us from arrogance and pride,
and teach us in Christ the greatness of humility
and service.

We make our prayer through our Lord Jesus
Christ, your Son,
who lives and reigns with you in the unity of
the Holy Spirit,
God for ever and ever.

YEAR B LORD our God,
you are the one God and there is no
other.

Give us grace to hear and heed
the great commandment of your kingdom,
that we may love you with all our heart
and love our neighbour as ourselves.

We make our prayer through our Lord Jesus
Christ, your Son,

who lives and reigns with you in the unity of
the Holy Spirit,
God for ever and ever.

YEAR C

JUST and merciful God,
true Lord of every house,
sure delight of every heart,
come into our midst today
to speak your word and satisfy our hunger.

Enable us to see you clearly,
to welcome you with joy,
and to give justice and mercy
a place in our lives.

Grant this through our Lord Jesus Christ, your
Son,
who lives and reigns with you in the unity of
the Holy Spirit,
God for ever and ever.

THIRTY-SECOND SUNDAY IN ORDINARY TIME

(The Sunday between 6 & 12 November inclusive)

YEAR A

BRIGHTEN your Church, O God,
with the promise of your kingdom
and waken our hearts to its light.
Bid us hasten with faith undimmed
to greet the bridegroom's return
and to enter the wedding feast.

We ask this through our Lord Jesus Christ,
your Son,
who lives and reigns with you in the unity of
the Holy Spirit,
God for ever and ever.

YEAR B

GOD, our provider,
you are the orphan's hope
and the widow's bread.

Strengthen our faith,
that with simplicity of heart
we may come to trust in you alone
and hold back nothing in serving you.

Grant this through our Lord Jesus Christ, your
Son,
who lives and reigns with you in the unity of
the Holy Spirit,
God for ever and ever.

YEAR C

GOD of all the living,
in the resurrection of Christ Jesus
you have given us the life
which even death cannot destroy.

Remember your unshakable promise
and strengthen us to live in this world
as your new creation.

We ask this through our Lord Jesus Christ,
your Son,
who lives and reigns with you in the unity of
the Holy Spirit,
God for ever and ever.

THIRTY-THIRD SUNDAY IN ORDINARY TIME

(The Sunday between 13 & 19 November inclusive)

YEAR A

O God,
from whose own abundance
all gifts and skills are lavishly bestowed,
encourage us to use our talents
as generously as you have allotted them,
so that, being faithful to your purpose,
we may become sharers in your glory.

We make our prayer through our Lord Jesus
Christ, your Son,
who lives and reigns with you in the unity of
the Holy Spirit,
God for ever and ever.

YEAR B

YOUR creation, O God,
runs its appointed course,
as from the ends of the earth
you gather a people you call your own.

Confirm us in the strength of your abiding
word.
Steady our hearts in the time of trial,
so that on the day of the Son of Man
we may without fear rejoice to behold his
appearing.

We ask this through our Lord Jesus Christ,
 your Son,
who lives and reigns with you in the unity of
 the Holy Spirit,
God for ever and ever.

YEAR C   LORD God of all the ages,
  the One who is, who was, and who is to
 come,
stir up within us a longing for your kingdom,
steady our hearts in time of trial,
and grant us patient endurance
until the sun of justice dawns.

We make our prayer through our Lord Jesus
 Christ, your Son,
who lives and reigns with you in the unity of
 the Holy Spirit,
God for ever and ever.

CHRIST THE KING

Last Sunday in Ordinary Time

(The Sunday between 20 & 26 November inclusive)

YEAR A

ALMIGHTY God,
you have conferred upon Christ Jesus
sovereignty over every age and nation.

Direct us, in the love of Christ,
to care for the least of his brothers and sisters,
that we may be subject to his dominion
and receive the inheritance of your kingdom.

Grant this through our Lord Jesus Christ, your
Son,
who lives and reigns with you in the unity of
the Holy Spirit,
God for ever and ever.

YEAR B

ALMIGHTY and eternal God,
to Jesus Christ, the first-born from the
dead,
you have granted everlasting dominion
and a kingship that shall not pass away.

Remove from us every desire for privilege and
power,
that we may imitate the sacrificial love of
Christ our King
and, as a royal and priestly people,
serve you humbly in our brothers and sisters.

Last Sunday in Ordinary Time

Grant this through our Lord Jesus Christ, your
    Son,
who lives and reigns with you in the unity of
    the Holy Spirit,
God for ever and ever.

YEAR C   GOD and Father of our Lord Jesus Christ,
        you gave us your Son,
the beloved one who was rejected,
the Saviour who appeared defeated.
Yet the mystery of his kingship illumines our
    lives.

Show us in his death
the victory that crowns the ages,
and in his broken body
the love that unites heaven and earth.

We ask this through our Lord Jesus Christ,
    your Son,
who lives and reigns with you in the unity of
    the Holy Spirit,
God for ever and ever.

Collects for Feasts
of the Lord and the Saints

FEASTS OF THE LORD AND THE SAINTS

2 FEBRUARY

THE PRESENTATION OF THE LORD

INSPIRED by your Spirit, Lord,
we gather in your temple to welcome your
Son.

Enlighten our minds
and lay bare our inmost thoughts.
Purify your people, and make us obedient to
the demands of your law,
so that we may mature in wisdom
and grow to full stature in your grace.

We ask this through our Lord Jesus Christ,
your Son,
who lives and reigns with you in the unity of
the Holy Spirit,
God for ever and ever.

19 MARCH

JOSEPH, HUSBAND OF THE VIRGIN MARY

O God,
   ever faithful to your covenant,
you strengthened Saint Joseph
to embrace the mystery of your will
and to welcome your Word, made flesh of the
   Virgin Mary.

Keep your Church also steadfast in faith,
ready to trust in your promises
and eager to fulfil your saving purpose.

We ask this through our Lord Jesus Christ,
   your Son,
who lives and reigns with you in the unity of
   the Holy Spirit,
God for ever and ever.

25 MARCH

THE ANNUNCIATION OF THE LORD

G OD most high,
   you extended your gracious mercy
to the whole human race
through your Son, Jesus Christ,
who took flesh of the Virgin Mary.

You gave him to the world as your servant,
whose delight was to do your will.
Keep the Church, which is his body,
faithful to your purpose,
that all the ends of the earth
may know your saving power.

Grant this through our Lord Jesus Christ, your
   Son,
who lives and reigns with you in the unity of
   the Holy Spirit,
God for ever and ever.

24 JUNE

THE BIRTH OF JOHN THE BAPTIST

VIGIL MASS

O God, you raise up prophets in every age.
Let your Spirit, who filled John the
Baptist from his mother's womb,
fill us with joy as we celebrate his birth.

May the example of his life,
the urgency of his preaching,
and the power of his prayers
make us ready to receive the one he
announced,
Jesus Christ, your Son,
who lives and reigns with you in the unity of
the Holy Spirit,
God for ever and ever.

MASS DURING THE DAY

GOD most high,
from his mother's womb you destined
John the Baptist
to preach repentance,
to challenge hardened hearts,
and so to herald salvation.

Grant us to embrace the conversion he
proclaimed
and to follow the one whose coming he
announced,
our Lord Jesus Christ, your Son,
who lives and reigns with you in the unity of
the Holy Spirit,
God for ever and ever.

29 JUNE

PETER AND PAUL, APOSTLES

VIGIL MASS

O God;
   source of every good gift
and sure foundation of our unity,
as we honour and revere Saints Peter and Paul,
grant your Church a share
in their zeal for preaching the gospel.
Strengthen our faith to be witnesses,
even unto death,
of the one Lord, Jesus Christ,
who lives and reigns with you in the unity of
   the Holy Spirit,
God for ever and ever.

MASS DURING THE DAY

L ORD, living God,
you crowned the faith of Peter
and the tireless preaching of Paul
with a share in Christ's triumphant death.

Renew our faith through their intercession
and, by the example of their lives,
rekindle our zeal for proclaiming the gospel.

Grant this through our Lord Jesus Christ, your
Son,
who lives and reigns with you in the unity of
the Holy Spirit,
God for ever and ever.

6 AUGUST

THE TRANSFIGURATION OF THE LORD

YEAR A

GOD of glory,
it is good for us to be here.

Reveal your Son to us now
in the message of the prophets
and the witness of the apostles,
that we may heed his voice
and receive him in faith.

We ask this through our Lord Jesus Christ,
your Son,
who lives and reigns with you in the unity of
the Holy Spirit,
God for ever and ever.

YEAR B

UPON a high mountain,
O God of majestic glory,
you revealed Jesus
in the mystery of his transfiguration
as your Son, the Beloved,
to whom we must listen.

By the word of his gospel,
shining for ever as a light in the darkness,
give us hope in the midst of suffering
and faith to perceive, even in the passion and
cross,
the glory of the risen Christ,

who lives and reigns with you in the unity of
   the Holy Spirit,
God for ever and ever.

YEAR C   GOD and Father of Jesus,
      you transfigured your Chosen One
and in heavenly light
revealed him as your Son.

Open our ears to the living Word
and our eyes to his glorious presence,
that we may be strengthened
in time of fear and uncertainty,
and one day pass over to share your glory.

Grant this through our Lord Jesus Christ, your
   Son,
who lives and reigns with you in the unity of
   the Holy Spirit,
God for ever and ever.

15 AUGUST

THE ASSUMPTION OF THE VIRGIN MARY INTO HEAVEN

VIGIL MASS

GRACIOUS God,
you chose the Virgin Mary
to bear your incarnate Word,
and at her life's end
you brought her in body and spirit to heavenly
glory.

Grant that, like Mary,
we may hear your word and keep it
and one day share with her
the risen life of Christ your Son,
who lives and reigns with you in the unity of
the Holy Spirit,
God for ever and ever.

Feasts of the Lord and the Saints

FAITHFUL to your promise, O God,
   you have lifted up the lowly,
clothing with heavenly splendour
the woman who bore Christ, our life and
   resurrection.

Grant that the Church, prefigured in Mary,
may bear Christ to the world
and come to share his triumph.

We ask this through our Lord Jesus Christ,
   your Son,
who lives and reigns with you in the unity of
   the Holy Spirit,
God for ever and ever.

14 SEPTEMBER

THE HOLY CROSS

LIFTED up among us, O God,
is Jesus the crucified:
sign of your steadfast love
and pledge of your will to save.

To those who look upon the cross with faith
grant healing of soul
and life eternal.

We ask this through our Lord Jesus Christ,
your Son,
who lives and reigns with you in the unity of
the Holy Spirit,
God for ever and ever.

1 NOVEMBER

ALL SAINTS

ALL-HOLY God,
you call your people to holiness.

As we keep the festival of your saints,
give us their meekness and poverty of spirit,
a thirst for righteousness,
and purity of heart.
May we share with them the richness of your
    kingdom
and be clothed in the glory you bestow.

Grant this through our Lord Jesus Christ, your
    Son,
who lives and reigns with you in the unity of
    the Holy Spirit,
God for ever and ever.

9 NOVEMBER

THE DEDICATION OF THE LATERAN BASILICA IN ROME

GOD all-holy,
in every place on earth
you gather your people into your presence
to proclaim the wonders of your love.

As we celebrate the dedication
of the cathedral church of Rome,
deepen our unity with your faithful throughout
the world,
and build us up into a house of prayer for all
nations.

We ask this through our Lord Jesus Christ,
your Son,
who lives and reigns with you in the unity of
the Holy Spirit,
God for ever and ever.

8 DECEMBER

THE IMMACULATE CONCEPTION OF THE VIRGIN MARY

GOD most high,
from the first moment of her conception
you favoured the Virgin Mary with your grace,
that she might become the mother of the
world's Redeemer.

As you blessed the daughter of Israel,
so grant us the grace
to be fully engaged in your service,
eager to do your will.
Hasten that day of gladness
when you will bring to completion your saving
work,
through Jesus Christ our Lord,
who lives and reigns with you in the unity of
the Holy Spirit,
God for ever and ever.